I0406980

BUSINESS LAW

PRACTICE

BY

BEN BOLFA

TABLE OF CONTENTS

CHAPTER

1

Legal Framework and Regulatory Bodies

PRINCIPAL LAWS & SUBSIDIARY LEGISLATIONS

- Companies & Allied Matters
- Companies proceedings rules
- Companies winding up Rules
- Investment & securities
- Securities & exchange commission rules
- Federal High Court Act
- Federal High Court Rules
- Investment promotion commission Act, national office for technology acquisition and promotion Act. Immigration act.
- Companies income tax Act
- Banks & other. Financial Institutions Act
- Federal Consumer and Consumer protection Act.
- Federal Inland Revenue Establishment act

TEST QUESTION

- MENTION OTHER LAWS

REGULATORY BODIES

- Corporate Affairs Commission.
- CAMA
- Status
- Membership
- Registrar- General

• Functions

FUNCTIONS OF CAC

- Administer the Act, regulation, supervision of the formation, incorporation,registration, management and winding up of companies.
- Establish a company's registry and offices in all the states of the federation.
- Arrange and conduct investigation into the affairs of companies in d interestsof shareholders and the public.
- Undertake other activities that are necessary to give full effect to the Act.
- Perform other functions as may be specified by any other Act or law.

ABC PLC

(Address)
• Internal Memorandum
• **To**: the Managing Director
• **From**: the Company secretary
• **Date**: May 22, 2023
• **Subject:** functions of the corporate affairs commission
- Thank you.
• Moe (Mrs.)
• Company secretary

Securities & exchange commission

- Body corporate
• Composition- chairman, dg, 3commissioners etc
• Tenure
- Functions of secretary

- Regulate investment & securities business.
- Register security exchanges, e.t.c
- Register securities of public companies
- Register and regulate corporate and individual capital market operators.
- Maintain register of foreign portfolio investment.

INVESTMENT PROMOTION COMMISSION

- Headed by a Secretary- Permanent Secretary in the civil service
- Tenure
- Governing Council- Chairman, Secretary, Gov Central Bank etc

Section 4
- Agency of Federal Government to co-ordinate and monitor all investment opportunities to which the Act Applies.
- Initiate and support measures to enhance investment climate in the country.
- Promote investment in the country
- Register& keep records of enterprise which the Act applies etc

NATIONAL OFFICE FOR TECHNOLOGY ACQUISITION AND PROMOTION COMMISSION.

- Functions?
- Effect of Non- Registration with not AP?

FINANCIAL REPORTING COUNCIL

SECTORS:
- Aviation
- Oil & Gas
- Communication
- Hotel & Tourism

- Power & Electric
- Financial Institutions
- Food & Drugs

ACCREDITATION – CAC

- Legal Practitioners, Chartered
Accountants, Chartered Secretaries

- PART A
- Note- First Directors, Subscribers can incorporate their own Companies.

PROCEDURE

- Accreditation Form
- 2 Passport Photographs
- Copy of Qualifying Cert.
- Practicing Fees
- Fee- This varies from country to country

REGISTRATION- CAPITAL MARKETOPERATOR

- Operators must Be registered
- Capital market Experts/ Professional

Legal Practitioners, Accountants, Auditors, Engineers, Estate Surveyors, PropertyManagers, & or Professionals as may be determined by the Commission.

REGISTRATION

Capital market experts or professionals to register as-
- Limited liability companies

- Firms & other Persons doing business in their true names.

FIRMS & PERSONS DOING BUSINESS IN THEIR TRUE NAMES

- CTC of bus. Name
- CV of the applicants
- Profile of the firm
- Partnership deed(if applicable)
- Postal address or electronic add of past employer.
- Sworn statement that requirement have been complied with.
- Annual practicing fees
- Proof indemnity insurance

Corporate bodies

- Sponsored application form
- Principal officer & Anor
- Curriculum Vitae of sponsored individuals
- Certificate of incorporation corporate bodies
- Sponsored application form
- form sec2- principal officer & Anor
- Curriculum Vitae of sponsored individuals
- Certificate of incorporation
- Evidence of minimum capital of 5million: This varies from country to country
- Profile of the co. – Past &present activities.
- ctc of me mart
- Audited accounts or statement of affairs- signed
- Postal add of. Sponsored individuals.
- Sworn undertaken to keep records.

QUALIFICATION

- Principal partners- 5yrs
- Sponsored officers – 2yrs

CHAPTER

2

CHOICE OF BUSINESS ORGANIZATION AND FORMATION

LEARNING OUTCOMES

- ✓ State the different types of business organizations that can be registered and advice on their features and suitability
- ✓ Prepare a checklist of documents required for registration of business organizations
- ✓ Conduct client interview and apply client instructions towards preparation ofdocuments for registration of business organizations.
- ✓ Identify the professional responsibilities involved

MEANING:
- A Business Organization is a going concern
- Profit – oriented
- Duly formed and incorporated/registered under the extant laws of a given country

TYPES OF BUSINESS ORGANIZATIONS

- Limited Liability Companies
- Sole Proprietorship
- Partnership
- Business Names

TYPES OF COMPANIES

- Company Limited by Guarantee
- Company Limited by Shares
- Unlimited Liability Company

- ✓ Any of the above Companies may be;
- A private company or
- A public company

COMPANY LIMITED BY GUARANTEE

- Shall not be registered with a share capital.
- The liability of the members to contribute to the assets shall not be less than $25 for instance. (This amount varies from country to country).
- Does not carry on business for the purpose of making profit for distribution as dividend to members.

Company Limited/Guarantee Cont'd

- May carry on limited Business to promote its aims and objectives.
- Formed to promote commerce, art, science, religion, sport, culture, education, research, charity or other similar objects.

UNLIMITED LIABILITY COMPANY

- An Unlimited Liability Company is a company not having any limit to the liability of its members.
- At liquidation, members are personally liable to the Company's indebtedness.

COMPANY LIMITED BY SHARE

- A Company limited by share is one that has the liability of its members at winding up limited to the amount, if any, unpaid on the shares held in the company.

- A Coy Ltd/Shares may create classes of shares as stipulated by law.

CHECKLIST OF COMPANIES

• A Company Ltd/Shares may be registered as:

1. Private company limited by shares
2. Public company limited by shares
3. Private company limited by guarantee
4. Public company limited by guarantee
5. Private unlimited companies
6. Public unlimited

FACTORS THAT MAY DETERMINE THE CHOICEOF BUSINESS ORGANIZATIONS

1. Nature of Business.
2. Available Capital
3. Number of members
4. Desired extent of liability of members
5. Commercial expediency.
6. The scope of operations.
7. Position of the Law/statutory requirements.
     E.g. Commercial Banks/Chambers of Commerce.
8. The cost of registration and expenses.
9. Speed of processing and completion of registration.
10. Post registration compliance issues.
11. The desire of the client himself

FEATURES OF A PRIVATE COMPANY

✓ It is stated in the Memo that it is a private company

- ✓ Authorized minimum share capital is $25 which varies from one country to another
- ✓ Every private company shall by its articles restrict the transfer of its shares.
- ✓ Members shall not exceed 50 except thee excess are persons in the bonafide employment of the company.
- ✓ Not required to hold statutory meeting or file statutory reports.
- ✓ Written resolutions can be passed by both Directors /members
- ✓ Public cannot subscribe its shares and debentures unless authorized by law.
- ✓ No restriction on the appointment of persons over 70 years as Directors.
- ✓ The company Secretary need not have certain professional qualifications.
- ✓ The removal of the Secretary does not require special procedures.
- ✓ No additional Notice.

WHEN RECOMMENDED

- • Where the capital available to start off business is relatively small
- • Where small and medium scale business organizations need to acquireincorporated status.
- • Where family and friends want to engage in business expected to last over a long period.

PECULIAR FEATURES OF A COMPANYLIMITED BY GUARANTEE

- ❖ The consent of the Attorney – General of the Federation must be obtained beforeits memo can be registered.
- ❖ It does not carry on business for the purpose of making profit to be distributed tomembers.
- ❖ It has no share capital.
- ❖ The liability of its members is upon winding up and where the company cannotsatisfy the debts.
- ❖ The numbers of people forming it must be clearly stated.
- ❖ Upon winding up, after the discharge of its debts, any assets the

company remaining shall not be distributed among the members but shall be transferred to some organization with similar objects.

❖ Its name must include the word "Limited by Guarantee" Ltd/Gte e.g. Chambersof Comm.

WHEN RECOMMENDED

• Where the company's object is for the promotion of commerce, art, science,religion, sports, culture, education, charity.

• Where the company's profit is not to be distributed to members as dividend.

• It is a subsidiary company set up to render corporate social responsibility,obligations for the parent company.

FEATURES OF A PUBLIC COMPANY

- It is stated in its memorandum to be a public company
- It can invite members of the public to subscribe to its shares and debentures
- It has the tendency of being larger and having more funds than many privatecompanies because they offer shares to the public
- It has an unlimited number of members
- The name ends with "Public Limited Company" Plc
- The authorized minimum share capital is $1500 (IT VARIES FROM ONE COUNTRY TO ANOTHER) and at least 25% of the share capital must be allotted to members at incorporation
- Where a person who is above 70 years is to be made a Director, specialnotice of his age must be given to the members in general meeting.
- It must hold its statutory meeting within 6 months of incorporation
- It must publish additional notice of its Annual General Meeting to itsmembers in Newspapers.
- The Secretary must be qualified.
- The removal of the company Secretary must accord with the

procedures lay down by law.

WHEN RECOMMENDED:

• Where the capital available to start off business is relatively large
• Where the business organization desires to have access to public funds throughoffering shares to the public for subscription
• Where membership is not limited or restricted Distinguishing between Private&Public
• Meeting
• Secretary
• Directorship
• Share Capital
• Resolution – written resolution
• Records and Returns
• Membership

Contrast Company Ltd/GTEE WITH Coy Limited/Shares

• Consent of Attorney General required for Company Ltd/Shares
• Distribution of Profit as Dividend
• Subscription clause/Undertaking and Special clause
• Authorized minimum Shares
• Tax Implication
• Dissolution and Winding up and Distribution of surplus assets

CLIENT INTERVIEW Quiz

Prepare a checklist of the questions to be asked during interview for formation of business org.

Client Interview Questionnaire

- Proposed Name of Company/ Alternative
- Registered Office Address/ Head Office
- Nature of Business
- Location
- What is the proposed sphere of coverage?
- How many members/shareholders/proprietors will you have for a start?
- What is the maximum number of members
- Ages of the persons forming the company
- Who are the Proposed Directors
- Any known legal disability
- Proposed minimum share capital
- Shareholding structure – Ratio
- Control and Management / Leverage on investment

GTE
- 1. What would be the extent of members undertaking to contribute
- 2. Name of the Company
- 3. What are the objects of business
- 4. Are the objects for promotion of commerce, art, science
- 5. Details of Subscribers
- 6. Permits and Approvals
- 7. What is the proposed NAME of the business
- 8. Control and Management
- 9. Raising and Borrowing Power
- 10. Registered Office Address.
- 11. Company Secretary
- 12. Directorship

1. Personal details
    Name in full ❖Nationality ❖ Gender ❖Age ❖Residential address
    Essentially to answer the question of
    capacity
2. Shareholders/ ownership

- How many persons to start up the business.
- ✔ membership
- ✔ Details of such members
- ✔ Nationality
- ✔ Age

3. Details of Directorship
- Who are to be Directors.
- ✔ Age

- ✔ Qualification = expertise
- ✔ Mental capacity
- ✔ Number of Directors
- ✔ Contact address

4. Sphere/dimension of Business

- Need for registered office address in Nigeria
- Leveraging on ECOWAS Protocol, WTO/GATT, etc
- Incentives - manufacturing and rural location

5. SHARES
- Share Capital
- Shares Allotment
- Types/Classes of Shares

6. **Restrictions on Power of the Company** Provides for full power
except curtailedin memo
- Borrowing Power of the Company to be expressly stated and with limitation if any.
- Biz and investment. Etc

7. Registered Office Address
- To capture details such as · Number · Street · Quarters/District · Town

8. Control and Management

• Use of Common Seal

  • Life Director
  • Chairman
  • Majority Shareholding
  • Preferential shareholding
  • Power to appoint and remove Director
  • Compulsory signatory to the account

9. Secretaryship
  • Details of Company Secretary
  • Qualification
  •etc

Type of company
• As envisaged.

11. The date for completion of registration

• Express service at CAC

NOT AVAILABLE AGAIN
▪ Professional Fees
▪ Commencement of Business
– after incorporation

12. Nature and objects of Business

·What is the nature of business? What are the objects of business? This will help the Solicitor to advice along

  a. Share capital prescription. e.g. banking, insurance, security, aviation, shipping,capital market, asset management
  b. need for proficiency certificate
  c. Obtaining needed permits, license, approval and consents.
  d. Regulatory agencies, Bodies, etc

13. Foreign Participation

- JVA
- Necessary permits from all respective bodies in a given country.
- Nature of the foreign participation FPI/FDI.
- Importation of Capital to avoid violation of money laundering statutes.

14. What is the proposed NAME of thebusiness Preferred name and Alternative Name

- **REGISTRABLE AND NON-REGISTRABLE NAMES**
  - **Conflicting Names**: Registered corporate Name

- **Restricted Names**: Names to be used subject to consent of CAC or solely reserved for a particular type of company
- **Prohibited Names**: Names that cannot be approved because of their illegal,offensive or deceptive nature.

Restricted name

- Cannot be registered except with the consent of CAC
- Names which contains the words "National", Government", "Municipal", "State", Federal", "Regional" which in the opinion of the CAC suggests or is calculated to suggest that it enjoys the patronage of the Federal/State Government. or any ministry or Contains the word "Municipal" or "Chartered" or in the opinion of CAC suggest connection with any municipal or other local authority;
- Contains the words " co-operative" or the words "Building secured
- Contains the word "Group" or "Holding"
- Name that contains the words "Chamber of commerce"

CHECKLIST OF PROHIBITEDCORPORATE NAMES

Either because such name conflict with an
1. Already registered
2. Reserved names or
3. Deceptive or

4. Illegal or offensive to public policy

DOCUMENTS TO BE SUBMITTED TO CAC FOR INCORPORATION OFCOMPANIES

Incorporation of companies limited by shares whether private, public or unlimitedcompany

THE STATUTORY FORMS

1. Availability Check and Reservation of Name
2. Now composite – embodies: ❑ Statement of Share Capitaland
Return of Allotment of Shares (duly stamped at the Stamp

Duties Office) ❑ Notice of Registered Office Address
   Declaration of compliance with the Requirement of   CAMA   (duly
      sworn to by Legal Practitioner before a Commissioner for Oaths/Notary
      Public)
❑ Particulars of Secretary of the Company
❑ Particulars of First Directors

OTHER DOCUMENTS/ITEMS

- Memorandum and Articles of Association (2printed and signed copies dulystamped at stamp Duties)
- Original receipts of CAC Filing/Registration fees, stamp duties andcompliance oath.
- Any otherDocument required by any other law /Regulation.

Incorporation of companies Limited by Guarantee

STATUTORY FORMS:

Availability and Reservation of name• (within 60 days ofreservation)
1. Duly completed;
- Declaration of Undertaking in compliance with the requirement of CAMA

- Particulars of first Directors

OTHER DOCUMENTS

- Memorandum and Articles of Association (With requisite special clauses &duly stamped; 2 copies)
- Letter of consent from the Attorney General of the Federation of a particular country.
- Receipt of CAC Filing fee and stamp duties for the memo and articles
- Any other Document required by any other law.

ETHICAL MATTERS

- Duty to act in good faith
- Duty to take full instruction.
- Duty to Disclose Conflicting Interest.
- The money collected must be disbursed in accordance with client's lawfulinstructions.
- Preserve Confidential Information.

It is the duty of the lawyer to devote his attention, energy and expertise to the service of his client.

CHAPTER
3

CORPORATE LAW PRATICE
CHOICES OF BUSINESS AND NON-BUSINESS ORGANISATION

- Partnership
- Company limited by guarantee
- Incorporated trustees

WHAT IS PARTNERSHIP?

 Partnership is the relationship which subsists between Persons carrying on business in common with a view of making profit.

CHARACTERISTICS OF PARTNERSHIP

- There must be business
- The business must be carried on in common by two or more persons
- The intention must be to make profit

CAPACITY OF PARTNERS

- Minors
- Persons of unsound mind
- Bankrupts
- Aliens

PARTNERSHIP AGREEMENT

- Oral
- Written
- By Deed

Necessity for formal Agreement

- Prevention of presumptions of law
- It forms a benchmark for reference time of crisis
- Easy enforceability of the terms
- Avoidance of bad faith, cheating and oppression

- Makes the terms easily ascertainable

CONTENT OF PARNERSHIP AGREEMENT

- Commencement: date; parties; addresses
- Names and Style of partners
- Payment of salaries
- Name and Style of Partnership (Note: prohibited and restricted names)
- Nature of business
- Place of business
- Capital of business
- Profits and losses
- Payment of salaries
- Management
- Duration
- Retirement
- Expulsion and Suspension
- Termination
- Banker and Signatories to account
- Drawings
- Insurance
- Limits of Authority
- Arbitration

Contrasting Partnership with Company

1. Legal Personality
2. Limitation of Liability
3. Number of Members
4. Management
5. Management
6. Formality and Publicity
7. Capital

8. Dissolution

COMPANY LIMITED BY GUARANTEE

What is Companies Limited by Guarantee
used for?Promotion of:
* Commerce
* Art
* Science
* Religion
* Sport
* Culture
* Education
* Research
* Charity

FEATURES OF A COMPANY LIMITED BY GUARANTEE

* Income and Property for the promotion of object only
* No distributable Profit
* Has no share capital
* Liability of members is limited to amount guaranteed/ undertaken (not <$25)
* Implementation of Liability delayed till occurrence of winding up
* Memo must contain Special Clause
* Assets not distributable upon dissolution
* Enjoys tax Exemption
* Consent of Attorney-General of Federation required for registration

NON-BUSINESS ORGANISATIONS INCORPORATED TRUSTEE
Incorporated Trustees may be

* Charitable bodies (i.e NGOs)
* Religious bodies
* Clubs

- Foundations
- Social associations
- Educational bodies
- Sporting associations, etc.

Appointment and Registration of Trustees

- One or more persons may be appointed
- Registration not mandatory
- It can legally carry out objectives of association prior to registration
- Unless registered the Trustee/ Trustees will not be a corporate body

Effects of Registration

The Trustee or Trustees become body corporate with:

- Perpetual succession
- Common seal
- Power to sue and be sued
- Power to hold and dispose property or any interest therein

Who cannot be a Trustee?

- An infant
- A person found by the court to be of unsound mind
- An undischarged bankrupt

COMPANY LIMITED BY GUARANTEE AND INCORPORATEDTRUSTEES DIFFERENCES AND SIMILARITIES

- Business and Non Business
- Special Clause
- Attachment of liability and Legal entity
- Profits not distributable
- Requirements of registration
- Requirements for registration
- Effects of registration
- Management

- Mode of Dissolution
- Application of Surplus assets upon dissolution.

PRACTICE QUESTONS

ANSWERS TO SCENARIO: CHOICE OF BUSINESS AND NON-BUSINESS ORGANIZATION AND FORMATION (PARTNERSHIP AND INCORPORATED TRUSTEES)

Nathan and Julius just got enrolled in the same high school and also proceeded to the same university where they met at California, their state of posting after the university education. During the service year, they started collecting and recycling plastic waste out of their passion for a clean and healthy environment. They eventually made a business out of it when they started supplying their recycled plastic to a plastic company in Florida and they want to run the business themselves with much ease because of their little resources. Still in pursuit of their passion for a clean environment, they started teaching people on how to properly dispose waste and creating awareness on the use of biodegradable materials for packaging goods and other products, they want this campaign to be a continuing one and to reach other parts of the country.

Answer the following questions:
1. Assuming you were engaged to register the business for them, what questions will you ask them during your meeting with them?

    a. The firm name and alternate name
    b. The general nature of business
    c. Postal address of the principal place of business and of any branches
    d. Full names of the individual proprietor or partners
    e. Full particulars of the principals
    f. Date of commencement of business

2. The documents you will require from them for registration are as follow:

- 2 Copies of Application Form

- Availability and Reservation of Name
- Passport photographs of each individual
- Registration Fee

3. The legal implications of the registered name upon registration are as follow:

   a. Registration does not give legal personality to the business or association but apprises the public of the true identity of the persons, who trade under the name.
   b. Registration gives priority to use of the name even against registered companies.
   c. Registration will not be construed as authorizing the use of the name, if apart from such registration; the use of the name could be prohibited.
   d. Registration is not proof of partnership. (supra) but raises a rebuttable presumption of the existence of partnership.

4. The name options available to them that will require no registration are as follow:

The true surnames of all partners without any addition other than, the trueforenames or the initials of the partners. The illustrations are as follows:

   a. Nathan Jones and Julius Shaw
   b. N. Jones and J. Shaw
   c. Jones and Shaw

5. Assuming they want to register the business as Nat and Jul CooperativeVentures, the implications is that::
   The Registrar may refuse to register the business name because the word 'Cooperative 'in the proposed name of the business falls under restricted unless the consent of Corporate Affairs Commission had been obtained. Restricted names are names which in the opinion of the Registrar of Corporate Affairs Commission is capable of misleading the public.
6. Three (3) presumptions that can be made as a result of their joint business are as follow::

a. Partnership Capital:

It will be presumed in the absence of a provision for capital contribution in the Partnership Agreement that the partners contributed the capital equally and must share the profit and losses equally.

b. Remuneration/Salary:

It will be presumed in the absence of a provision for payment of salary/remuneration in the Partnership Agreement that the partners will not be entitled to receive salary/remuneration.

c. Profit and Loss Sharing:

It will be presumed in the absence of a provision for profit and loss sharing in the Partnership Agreement that the profit and loss will be equally shared by the partners.

d. Expulsion:

It will be presumed in the absence of a provision for expulsion in the Partnership Agreement that the partners lack the power to expel any partner. If they attempt to expel any partner, the partnership stands dissolved.

e. Partnership Property:

It will be presumed that the partners have equal rights to the partnership property if nothing is provided on the contrary in the Partnership Agreement.

f. Dissolution of Partnership:

The partnership will be presumed to be partnership-at-will which can be dissolved at the instance of any of the partners (notice). Death, incapacity, expulsion or resignation of a partner may also signify the dissolution of the partnership if there is no provision in the Partnership Agreement for continuation of the partnership after such occurrences.

7. Five clauses that will be included in the agreement that will regulate their joint business are as follow::

a. Parties
b. Name and style
c. Place of business
d. Nature of business
e. Commencement
f. Duration
g. Capital
h. Property of Partnership
i. Profits and drawings
j. Bankers and signatories to bank account
k. Salary/Remuneration
l. Accounts
m. Powers, rights and duties
n. Retirement
o. Expulsion and Suspension
p. Dissolution
q. Arbitration

8. The appropriate form of registration for their campaign on a clean environment is to register Incorporated Trustees. This is because the aims and objectives of the organization they want to form is to educate the entire people of Nigeria on how to properly dispose waste and creating awareness on the use of biodegradable materials for packaging goods and other products, as well as the organization being a non-profit organization falls.:

"where one or more trustees are appointed by any community of persons bound together by custom, religion, kinship or nationality or by anybody or association of persons established for any religious, **educational**, literary, scientific, social, development, cultural, sporting or charitable purpose, he or they may, if so authorized by the community, body or association (in this Act referred to as "the association") apply to the Commission in the manner hereafter provided for registration under this Act as a corporate body".

9. The steps involved in getting the body registered are as follow::

   a. Taking instructions
   b. Holding of meeting of the body where the trustees are appointed andthe Special Clause adopted
   c. Writing of letter authorizing the person handling the registration
   d. Conduct availability check and reservation of name
   e. Publication in two (2) daily newspapers of which one must be circulating in the local area and the other one circulating nationally, calling for objection within 28 days
   f. Preparation of incorporation documents (filling of application form, constitution, Trustee Declaration Form, obtaining passport photographs of trustees, etc)
   g. Preparation of the Common Seal of the body
   h. Formal application addressed to the Registrar-General, of the Corporate Affairs Commission requesting for his consent/approval for the registration of the body by the person registering the body
   i. Payment of filling fees
   j. Filing
   k. Obtaining the certificate of incorporation and CTCs of the constitutionand application form of the body.

10. The person that may join in the registration of the body must be:

   a. An adult
   b. A person of sound mind
   c. A person who is not bankrupt
   d. A person who has not been convicted of an offence involving fraud or dishonesty within five (5) years of his proposed appointment.

11. The minimum number of person that is registered for the body to have corporate personality is one person. This also provides that one or more trustees are required for registration of an

Incorporated Trustees.

12. The documents required for registration of the body are as follows:

a. Form of approval of name
b. Duly completed set of Incorporation Form
c. Trustees Declaration Form
d. Formal application letter for registration signed by the chairman and secretary
e. Extracts of minutes of general meeting appointing trustees and adoptingspecial clause in the constitution signed by the chairman signed by the chairman and secretary
f. Two printed copies of the constitution
g. Trustees declaration from duly deposed to by each trustee in the High Court
h. Impression of the common seal of the association on the application form
i. Payment of filing fee
j. Evidence of newspaper publication of advertisement of trustees
k. Impression of common seal
l. Evidence of land ownership
m. Two passport photograph of each Trustees
n. Letter authorising the Solicitor handling the registration

13. Five (5) provisions that must be contained in the constitution of the body areas follows:

a. Name
b. Aims and objectives
c. Common seal
d. Special clause
e. Trustees
f. Governing body
g. Meetings
h. Accounts

PRE-INCORPORATION MATTERS & PROMOTION ACTIVITIES

Word of Wisdom

Successful people have fear; successful people have doubts, and have worries: they just don't let these feelings stop them. So don't allow fear, self-doubt and worries stop your dreams.

AND THE WORK FOR TODAY

- Promotion Of Companies
  &
- Pre –Incorporation Contracts

LESSON OUTCOME

- ➢ State the relevance of promotion activities and duties of promoter.
- ➢ Discuss the incidences, types and features of pre-incorporation contracts(Joint venture and Shareholders agreement.).
- ➢ Discuss the relationship between MEMART & pre-incorporation contract
- ➢ List the contents of Shareholders Agreement, JVA and CommercialMemorandum of Understanding
- ➢ Draft Pre-incorporation Contracts.
- ➢ Identify ethical issues involved in pre-incorporation matters.

CONTENT

- 1. Promotion and Nature of Promotion activities and duties of promoter.
- 2. Types and feature of different pre-incorporation contracts (Joint ventureand Shareholders Agreements)
- 3. Drafting of Pre-incorporation contract

- 4. Ethical issues involved

COMPARING A PROMOTER

1. Nurse/Mid Wife
2. Concert and Event Planner
3. A Forerunner

PROMOTION OF A COMPANY

- For a company to come into existence there must be persons who wouldpromote and float it.
- Promotion activities usually involve

I. Fund raising

II. Obtaining requisite permits

III. Packaging of incorporation documents

IV. Land acquisition

V. Personality Shopping/Employment/Staffing etc.

WHO IS A PROMOTER?

- **A** promoter is any person who takes part in forming a company or undertakes a given project or takes steps to accomplish the purpose of a newly formed company or participates in raising funds for a newly incorporated company.

WHAT OF PROFESSIONALS ENGAGED IN COMPANY FORMATION?

- But a person who acted in a professional capacity and was briefed by the Promoter is not a promoter.
- Accountant who prepares financial analysis or a solicitor who prepares the memorandum and articles and registers the company for client and is paid his professional fees is not a promoter.

They may not be Promoters:

- Solicitor
- Engineer
- Architect
- Surveyor
- Estate Agent. etc
- The court set up a test of determining who is a promoter, thus:
- " A promoter is one who undertakes to form a company with reference to a given object and set it going and who takes necessary steps to accomplish that purpose"

QUERIES: PLS NOTE

However, A Professional Who Does Beyond His Professional Engagement May Be Treated As A Promoter.
- For Instance, A Lawyer Who After Incorporation, Assist In Employment,Securing Accommodation, Personality Shopping, Equipments, Etc.

Principles

- A promoter is not a trustee or an agent.
- A company as a corporate body may promote another company.

LEGAL RELATIONSHIP BETWEEN A PROMOTER & THE COMPANY

- A promoter stands in a fiduciary relationship to the company thus must observe utmost good faith towards the company in any transaction with it or on its behalf.
- Where he fails to observe utmost good faith, the promoter shall be liable to compensate the company for any loss incurred.

DUTIES OF PROMOTERS

a) Duty to account for money/ properties received in the course of the promotion activities

b) He must disclose any property or information which is acquired on behalf of the company especially where he has used the information or property to gain a benefit.

c) Duty to disclose conflicting interest in transactions with the company
d) Duty not to expose the company to loss.
e) Duty not to make secret profit; where made, it must be refunded to the company.

LIABILITIES OF PROMOTERS

Where there is a breach of the duties imposed on a promoter, the company cantake any of the following actions for redress

i. Action to render account of money or property received in the course ofpromotion activities
ii. Action to account for secret profit made
iii. Action for damages for wrongful exploitation of confidential information
iv. Refusal to ratify pre-incorporation contract tainted with conflict of interest
v. Action to refund.
vi. Rescission (strongest tool)

REASON FOR RESCISSION

- A promoter is in a fiduciary relationship to the company, thus any breach of this duty entitles the company to rescission from such contracts.

IS THE RIGHT OF RESCISSION OF A COMPANY ABSOLUTE?

- NO, it is not absolute.
- The court may in its equitable jurisdiction stop a company from rescission.

For instance, a company may not rescind where there is full disclosure of material facts known by the promoter and the contract has been ratified on behalf of the company.

Where rescission not possible, the company may take option of Recovery of Profit

- Where it is not possible for the company to rescind the contract the companymay recover the profit made in the transaction.
- Sometimes, recovering profit only may not be sufficient thus company isentitled to sue for damages for the breach of the fiduciary duty.
- Also, a subscriber has a right to sue for damages where he relied on the falseinformation given to him by the promoter subscribing for the shares

Is there Limitation of time in action against a promoter?

- ❖ Action against a promoter by a company is not limited by time.
- ❖ But the court has the discretion to relieve a promoter in whole part fromliability considering the circumstances and lapse of time.

RATIFICATION OF CONTRACT ENTERED BY PROMOTER

a. By the company's Board of directors independent of the promoter
b. By all the members of the company; or
c. By the company at a general meeting at which neither the promoter shareholders of any shares in which he is beneficially interested shall vote on the resolution to enter into or ratify the transaction.

REMUNERATION OF PROMOTERS

- ❑ A promoter has no right against the company for payment of services rendered before incorporation.
- ❑ The law is that unless the company's Articles of Association permits the Directors to pay, a promoter is not entitled to remuneration for services secured as a promoter.
- ❑ Where the promoter enters into a contract with the proposed

company he canrecover his fees and preliminary expenses where the contract is ratified by the company.

Issues of Remuneration Generally?

I. Promoter
II. Executive director
III. Managing director
IV. Non – executive director
V. Trustees
VI. Company secretary

The forms of Remuneration available to a Promoter:

1. He may negotiate on behalf of the company for a sale / purchase but withcommission.
2. He may also take shares which are to be credited as fully paid.
3. He may be paid agency fees
4. He may be given appointment as director.
5. The promoter may purchase a property and sell it to the company at inflatedprice = profits.

Consequence of a promoter convicted of fraudulent practices in the course of promotion

- Where a person has been convicted by a court for any offence in connection with the promotion or formation of a company he may be barred/suspended from being a director or from taking part in the management of any company for a period **not exceeding 10 years** as may be specified by the court.

PRE-INCORPORATION CONTRACTS

- Pre-incorporation contracts entered into by person on behalf of a company before its incorporation.

Gestation contracts

- Pre-incorporation contracts such as promotion agreements, preliminary agreements formation agreements, shareholders agreement, memorandum of undertaking, Pre-incorporation agreements etc

LEGAL STATUS OF PRE-INCORPORATION CONTRACTSPOSITION AT COMMON LAW

- At Common law, a company is not bound by contracts purported enteredinto on its behalf by its promoters or other persons before incorporation. Andthe company cannot, after incorporation ratify or adopt such a contract. **Common law position**
- The rationale is that since a company has no legal existence before incorporations, it is incapable of entering into a contract itself and also incapable of acting through an agent. - **KELNER V. BAXTER**
- It was held that where a contract is signed by a person as "agent" but who has no principal existing at that time, the contract would be wholly inoperative, binding upon the person who signed it.
- A stranger cannot relive him of the liability by subsequent ratification.
- See also **Leopold New Borne (London) Ltd v. Sensolid (Great Britain) Ltd**
- In that case, the court further held that to be able to enjoy the benefits of a pre-incorporation agreement. The company ought to have entered into a fresh agreement upon the same terms of the previous one after its incorporation.

WHAT IS THE LEGAL REGIME UNDER CAMA?

- A company upon incorporation can ratify all the pre-incorporation contracts entered on its behalf. Thus, the company becomes bound and is entitled to the benefits and obligations thereto.
- However, before such ratification, the person (or promoter) who

purported to act in the name or on behalf of the company shall be personally bound by the contract or transaction and entitled to the benefits and obligations thereof

- The Supreme Court confirmed the provides that ratification of pre-incorporation contracts in the case of Society Generale Bank (Nig) Ltd v. Society General Favouraiser

Right to Rescind

- A company has a right to rescind from any contract entered into on its behalf before its incorporation. However, this right of rescind must be applied considering and according with the general principles of law on rescission ofcontracts.

CONFLICT BETWEEN PROVISIONS OF MEMART & PRE-INCORPORATION CONTRACT

- Where there is a conflict between the memo and articles on one hand and the pre-incorporation contract on the other hand, the provision of the memorandum & articles shall prevail.

- Even where a "Supremacy clause" is inserted into the pre-incorporation contract, it would still not go to erode the clear provision of the CAMA which in Section 41(1) describes the memo and articles as superior contract of the company.

EFFECTS OF PRE-INCORPORATION CONTRACT ON THEMEMORANDUM AND ARTICLES OF ASSOCIATION

- The inclusion of the terms of a pre-incorporation contract in the object clause is the intention to carry out such objects.

- PLS NOTE, the inclusion of a pre-incorporation contract in the MEMO of a company does not impose extra liability on the COY, but amounts to no more than a serious desire by the promoters that the proposed coy after its formation should execute the terms of the contract.

- Provisions made in the Articles of Association on rules of management of the company, the management and members of the company are bound to observe them.

TYPES OF PRE-INCORPORATION CONTRACTS

- Joint venture agreement
- Shareholder's agreement
- Contract for payment of promoter's expenses
- Directors' service contract
- Contract for conversion of partnership into incorporated company
- Contract for acquisition of property.
- Contract of Transfer of Technology.

CONTENTS OF SHAREHOLDERS AGREEMENT

- Parties and their capacities, Date, Recital, Consideration, Registered office, Companies business, Dividend policies, Directors, Secretary Auditors and Bankers, Warranties, Guarantees and indemnities, Financing Accounts, Transfer of shares and loans, Restrictive covenants, Procedure to resolve Deadlock, Important management decisions, Confidentiality, Dispute Resolution, pre emptive rights, Winding up Shareholders consent etc

JOINT VENTURE AGREEMENT

- A joint venture Agreement is more specific and formal than the Memorandum of Understanding in terms of binding and enforceable terms.
- At this stage, parties are certain as to the terms of the venture.
- This also contains consideration or contributions.
- It is not unusual to find clauses in the MOU also in the JVA.

CONTENT OF JOINT VENTURE AGREEMENT

- Parties and their description, Date, Recital
- Nature of business, Registered office
- Dividend policies, Financing accounts
- Confidentiality, Restrictive covenants
- Directors and Secretary, Winding up
- Consideration, Dispute Resolution, applicable law, capital

contribution,admission of new partner, transfer of technology, etc

- Sample draft of Resolution for Ratification/Adoption of Promoter contract.

CHAPTER

5

FOREIGN PARTICIPATION

Overview

- Categories of Foreigners
- Incorporate a Nigerian company
- legal regulatory framework
- Register with NIPC
- Import Capital
- Assurances
- Licence, Approval
- Incentives;

INTRODUCTION

- A foreigner is free to do business alone or in partnership with any otherperson.

Negative list

- Prohibition:
- to everybody (negative list):
- Production of arms, ammunition etc;
- Production of and dealing in narcotic drugs and psychotropic substances;
- Production of military and paramilitary wears including those of the police,customs, immigration and prison.

Categories - "Foreign Investors (FIs)"

Foreign Institutional Investors (FIIs) Foreign Portfolio investors (e.g. pension fund managers, unit trust investment managers, institutional portfolio managers registered in other jurisdiction(s), who buy into a company in a particular country without actual participation:

1. Direct investors who invest in the Country's market (primary or secondary)with foreign currency.
2. Individual Investors who are foreigners and citizen of a country resident abroad...

…who are investing with foreign currency.

3. A foreign company could also be exempted from registration upon an application to the President by virtue of a treaty to which a country is a party.

Portfolio investors

- Securities and Exchange Commission
- Foreign companies in a given country for a specific purpose can apply to the President for exemption from registration

LEGAL REGULATORY FRAMEWORK

- IMMIGRATION ACT

- Foreign Exchange (Monitoring & Miscellaneous Provisions)
- National Office for Technology Acquisition and Promotion

- Industrial Inspectorate

- Companies Income Tax

- Personal Income Tax

OVERVIEW

- A foreign company must first register as a separate entity before they can operate: until incorporated, it cannot carry on any business in a particular country or exercise any of the powers of a registered company.
- It cannot even have a place of business for service of documents or processes in a particular country, except receipt of documents as a prelude to incorporation.

Consequence of non-compliance

- If Foreign coy does not register, any transaction entered into is void and illegal
- The court will therefore not enforce the contract at the instance of any party to the transaction:
- Can a party at wrong use the section as a sword or defence?

- Unlikely to sue if he has benefitted but if the aggrieved party sues on it the court will not allow the party who is wrong to raise the illegality as a defence.

Can a foreign company sue or be sued in a particular Country?

- Yes
- **Ritz Pumenfabrlk GMBH & Co KG v Techno Continental EngineersNig. Ltd (1999) 4 NWLR 298.**
- **NBCI v Europa Traders (U.K.) Ltd (1990) 6 NWLR 36**
- **Watanmal (Singapore) Pte Ltd. Vs. Liz Olofin and Company Plc [1998]1 NWLR pg 311**
- **Fabno Industries Limited v United Distillers Plc. (1999) 5 NWLR (Pt.602) 314**

Exempted companies

- A company may also be exempted under a treaty to which a country is a party.
- Foreign companies in another country for a specific purpose can apply to the President for exemption from registration
- These companies are:
- foreign companies invited to another country by or with the approval of the Federal Government to execute any specified individual project;
- foreign companies which are in a particular country for the execution of specific individual loan projects on behalf of a donor country or international organization;
- Foreign government-owned companies engaged solely in export promotion activities and
- Engineering consultants and technical experts engaged on any individual specialist project

Application for exemption

- An application for exemption from registration as a company in a country is addressed to the Secretary to the Federal Government:
- However, the application is considered and given by the President

Application for exemption docs +info to attach

- a. The name of the company
- Address outside the country.
- The proposed company name in Nigeria
- Address in a particular country
- Names of directors
- Attach CTC of memart of the company
- Are there representatives of a country?
- Disclose the proposed business in the country.

- Have they previously carried on any business as exempted foreign company?

Period of Exemption
- Where exemption is granted, the company is given an exemption order.
- It is granted for a specified period.

Revocation of exemption
- The President may revoke the exemption if he is of the opinion that the company has contravened the corporate body or has not fulfilled any condition of the exemption order or for any good or sufficient reason.
- Annual report shall disclose the following -
  (1) Place/country of registration
  (2) Date of registration and certificate number
  (3) Principal place of business in place/country of registration
  (4) Share capital of the company (if any)
  (5) Principal place of business in a particular country
  (6) Date of exemption
  (7) Description of business in a country
- (8) Expected date of completion of business in a particular country
  (9) Name and address of each director, partner or other principal officers of the company since date of exemption and any changes therein
- Companies Regulations (as amended)

Status of an exempted company
- It has the status of an unregistered company.

Registration Process
- Registration Process at the Corporate Affairs Commission (already discussed) first before anything else
- In the meantime, Draft Joint venture agreement if in

partnership witha particular person/a given country company.

Application by Foreign investor

- A foreign investor must, after incorporation as a company in a particular country but before starting business, apply to the corporate body incharge on the prescribed form for registration
- The corporate body has a Governing Council consisting of a Chairman, a representativeeach from some Federal Ministries: and
- An Executive Secretary

Application to Corporate Body

- This body is the agency of Government that co-ordinates and monitors all investment promotion activities. It houses One Stop Investment Centre (OSIC). This body varies from country to country.
- One Stop Investment Centre(OSIC) is an agency that helps foreigners tointerface with agencies like Immigration CAC, SEC,
- Foreigner can choose to apply directly to those Agencies

Functions of Corporate body

- Registers all foreign investors
- Promotes investments in and outside of the country through effective promotionalmeans
- Identifies specific projects and invite interested investors for participation inthose projects
- Disseminates information about investment opportunities in the country
- Disseminates up to date information on incentives available to investors;
- provides support services;
- organizes exhibitions conferences and seminars
- Advises Government on policy matters to promote development of the economy
- Performs such other functions as are supplementary or

incidental to the attainment of the objectives of the Act

Documents to accompany the application to the Corporate body

- Government treasury receipt evidencing the purchase of body Form;
- Certificate of Incorporation
- Tax Clearance Certificate
- Memorandum and Articles of Association;
- Receipts of stamp duty on the authorized share capital of the company
- Formal Application Letter to Executive Secretary of Corporate body
- Memorandum and Articles of Association;
- Receipts of stamp duty on the authorized share capital of the company
- Formal Application Letter to Executive Secretary of Corporate body
- Evidence of having sourced the plant and machinery to be used in the company's business;
- Deed(s) of Sub-Lease/Tenancy Agreement for the premises to be used forthe company's operation.
- A list of the directors of the company; and their particulars / theirnationalities;
- Job title designations of expatriate quota positions required, and CVs ofpeople proposed for employment

After submission

- The Corporate body to register within 14 working days from receiving a completed registration or otherwise advises the applicant.

Certificate of Capital Importation

- Having submitted the documents to Corporate body (this varies from country to country), the foreign company (company in a particular country) must then import its foreign equity through an authorized bank and obtain a Certificate of Capital Importation (CCI) from the bank. This is then taken to NIPC as part of documents.
- The capital importation could be in cash, consideration other than cash, e.g. importation of equipment or raw materials, or through the Debt equity conversion programme (see later).

Advantages of Certificate of Capital Importation CCI

- Entitles the foreign investor to:
- Open a foreign currency Dorm Account with any authorised dealer:
- Open a special non-resident account (with the currency of a given country)
- Buy shares in a country's companies out of the account (with the currency of a given country).
- Repatriate the capital, dividends and incomes at autonomous market rates minus taxes.

Acquisition of a foreign enterprise and payment of compensation
- No enterprise shall be nationalized or expropriated by the Federal Government, unless the acquisition is in the national interest or for public purpose

Consequence of expropriation
- Payment of compensation; and a right of access to the courts as to quantumof compensation
- Compensation to be paid promptly and in foreign exchange

Dispute settlement procedures

- 1st by mutual discussion to reach an amicable settlement.
- Dispute between an investor of a country and Government - the rules of procedure for arbitration are in the Arbitration and Conciliation or
- Dispute between a foreign investor and Government
- Does a country have any bilateral or multilateral treaty with the country of the investor?
- If so then they can use any machinery for settlement of investment disputes agreed on by the parties.

- **Investment promotion and protection agreement**
- An Investment Promotion and Protection Agreement IPPA provide the baseline minimum protections for foreign investments.
- So in case of dispute between foreigner and Govt. of a country you could use provisions of the IPPA for resolution

IPPA -countries

China, Finland, France, Germany, Italy, Korea Republic, Netherlands, Romania, Singapore, South Africa, Spain, Algeria, Sweden, China, Finland, France, Germany, Italy, Korea Republic, Netherlands, Romania, Singapore, South Africa, Spain, Algeria, Sweden,

ICSID- INTERNATION CENTRE FOR SETTLEMENT OF INVESTMENT DISPUTES

- For other countries with no treaty or investment protection agreement with a particular country, you look at rules made by International Centre for Settlement of Investment Disputes (ICSID)

One Stop Investment Centre

- This is an investment facilitation mechanism where relevant government agencies are brought to one location, coordinated and streamlined, to provide efficient and transparent services to investors

Foreign Exchange (Monitoring And Misc. Provisions)

- Foreign currency held or imported by – citizens of a country home and abroad, Foreigners resident in in a country;
- Nobody is required to declare any foreign currency at the port of entry into a country unless its value is in excess of US $5,000 or its equivalent and even then, the amount that is declared is for statistical purposes only.
- See Money Laundering (Prohibition) (Amendment) Act.
- Forfeiture of undisclosed funds or negotiable instrument or to imprisonment of not less than 2 years or to both.
- Amount increased to $10000
- Agency commissions, professional fees and other forms of invisible earnings;
  - Non-oil export proceeds earned by exporters of a country goods;
  - Foreign currency held by citizens of a particular country resident in that same country;
  - Foreign currency imported or held by foreign Embassies, and international organizations from external sources;
  - Foreign currency provided by the Central Bank;

- Foreign currency imported for direct or portfolio investment in a country; and
- Foreign currency from such other sources as the Minister may, from time totime, specify by order published in the *Gazette.*

Debt-equity programme

- Capital can be brought into the country through the debt-equity programme of the federal government, whereby a country's debt instrument is bought at a discounted value from any stock exchange anywhere in the world the foreigninvestor will get the currency equivalent of a country of the face value of the instrument
- It is implemented by the DMO later renamed DMB

Participation

- To participate a company must have a minimum paid-up capital of $5,000.
- the minimum amount of debt to be considered under the Scheme shall be $250,000

ELIGIBLE PARTICIPANTS

- Companies and individuals, citizens and non- citizens
- Residents and non-residents

REPATRIATION OF INCOME

- The repatriation of the profits/capital dividends derived from the initialcapital outlay can be done at any time

Ease of doing business in a country

- The Federal Government of a county put in place policies affecting the ease of doing business in the country, support for local content, and timely submission of annual budgetary estimates by all government agencies.
- Undoubtedly these policies increased our ranking in the Ease of Doing Business Index in the world.

Executive Orders

- Visas must be issued or rejected with reason by the Consular Office of a country Embassies and High Commissions within 48 hours of receipt of valid application.
  - Government agencies are required to publish a complete list of all requirements for obtaining permits, licences and approvals, including fees and timelines, in their premises and on their websites
  - They are required to streamline all activities e.g at the airport instead of a foreigner to be subjected to scrutiny by Immigration or Customs etc. The different regulatory agencies at the airports are mandated to merge their respective departure and arrival interfaces into a single customer interface.
  - An application is deemed granted if after a certain period, he does not hear from the government agency he can then at the expiration of the application period apply to the supervising Minister to issue any document or certificate required

TYPES OF VISA pre 2020.
- Transit
- Diplomatic
- Business
- Tourist
- Temporary work permit (TWP)
- Subject to regularisation (STR)

Visa Policy
- Introduction of 3 categories of visas and
- expansion of visa classes from 6 to 79
- Introduction of e-visa
- The New Visa classes include:
- **28 New Short Term Visas(STV) Classes: - 3months**
- 36 New Temporary Residence Visas Classes: **two years, (TRV)and**
- 15 New Permanent Residence Visas
- **STV - tourism, study tour, academic exchange program, humanitarianservices, relief/emergency works and temporary work permit**
- Note that STR has now been renamed Temporary Residence Visas

Classes:
- 36 New Temporary Residence Visas Classes: **two years,** multiple entry visa
- 15 New Permanent Residence Visas Classes: highly skilled individuals aswell as some categories of retirees.
- Permanent Residence Visa (PRV)
- This status can be conferred on spouses of citizens of a country, by birth who have renounced their citizenship, and their spouses,

www.ingramcontent.com/pod-product-compliance
Lightning Source LLC
Chambersburg PA
CBHW062300290526
45794CB00006B/2640